Plymouth ROCKS!

To Yo, her book—J. Y.

For Amelia and Leo—S. S.

At the time of publication, all URLs printed in this book were accurate and
active. Charlesbridge, the author, and the illustrator are not responsible for
the content or accessibility of any website.

Published by Charlesbridge
9 Galen Street
Watertown, MA 02472
(617) 926-0329
www.charlesbridge.com

Printed in China
(hc) 10 9 8 7 6 5 4 3 2 1

Library of Congress Cataloging-in-Publication Data
Names: Yolen, Jane, author. | Streed, Sam, illustrator.
Title: Plymouth rocks: the stone-cold truth / Jane Yolen; illustrated by Sam
   Streed.
Description: Watertown, MA: Charlesbridge, [2020] | Written for the 400th
   anniversary of the Pilgrims landing in Massachusetts. | Includes
   bibliographical references. | Summary: In humorous verse Plymouth Rock
   tells the story of itself, from glacial erratic to national icon—with historical
   asides and corrections by a fact checker.
Identifiers: LCCN 2019008772 (print) | LCCN 2019010852 (ebook) | ISBN
   9781580896856 (hardcover) | ISBN 9781632898326 (ebook)
Subjects: LCSH: Historic sites—United States—Juvenile fiction. | National
   monuments—United States—History—Juvenile fiction. | Stories in
   rhyme. | Humorous stories. | Plymouth Rock (Plymouth, Mass.)—Juvenile
   fiction. | Plymouth (Mass.)—History—Juvenile fiction. | CYAC: Stories in
   rhyme. | Plymouth Rock (Plymouth, Mass.)—Fiction. Massachusetts—
   History—Fiction. | Humorous stories. | LCGFT: Stories i rhyme. |
   Humorous fiction.
Classification: LCC PZ8.3.Y76 Pl 2020 (print) | LCC PZ8.3.Y76 (ebook) |
   DDC 813.54 [E]—dc23
LC record available at https://lccn.loc.gov/2019008772
LC ebook record available at https://lccn.loc.gov/20190108522

Illustrations doodled on paper, scanned, finished, and colored digitally
Display type set in Old Claude by LetterPerfect Design
Text type set in Lazy Vermont by Lazy Dog Foundry
Color separations by Colourscan Print Co Pte Ltd, Singapore
Printed by 1010 Printing International Limited in Huizhou, Guangdong, China
Production supervision by Brian G. Walker
Designed by Diane M. Earley and Sam Streed

Plymouth ROCKS!

The Stone-Cold Truth

Jane Yolen • Illustrated by Sam Streed

Charlesbridge

Rock Speaks

You know that I'm old,
and rather well known.
But everything told
is not set in stone.

Two kinds of history.
Not all of it true.
Not all of it false.
It's now up to you.

Research and study,
discuss, and choose.
Some call it fiction.
Some call it news.

Rock

Rock & Roll

I was not born where I was found.
In fact I wandered all around.
Erratic, I am sometimes called.
A glacial friend just let me fall,
left me there and moved away.
I haven't seen it since that day.
(I really hope that it's okay!)

A glacial erratic rock is one that was moved by a glacier.
Plymouth Rock is a granodiorite, a rock similar to granite.
More than six hundred million years ago, Rock was part of a
larger granodiorite that was carried away by a glacier. When
the glacier melted, Rock dropped off and got left behind.

Rock Bottom

A few years later—eons, they say—
woolly mammoths came my way.
Rubbed their tails on my backside.
My, those creatures sure were wide.

Rock almost gets a pass on this one. Woolly mammoths did come across the Bering Strait to North America. Though most of their bones have been found in the Dakotas, a few remains of mammoths have been found closer to the East Coast.

A couple of mammoth teeth have actually been unearthed in Cape Cod. So maybe one or two wandered that far? Or maybe their fossilized bones got dropped by some kind of erratic rock. We just don't know yet.

Rock Band

For a long while, just creature comforts:
deer and elk galore.
An occasional snake for shivers' sake,
though after a while it, too, proved a bore.
A stone's life has but few adventures.
A rock, a roll—and little more.

Rock Solid

Native people fished nearby me.
Their children sometimes tried to climb me.
Their fires kept me warm and toasty,
cooking dinners that were roasty.
But alas, I do not eat,
and so I never tasted meat.

I am a rock-a-tarian.

Rocking the Boat

New men and women passing by
on occasion caught my eye.
Their color, clothes, and tongue seemed strange.
Even a Rock can note that change.
Different people, same old ground.
An old world lost. A new one "found."

Rock is missing a lot of detail here. Settlers didn't just "find" a new world, they colonized it. After taking over the southern part of the East Coast, many English, French, and Spanish settlers traveled north.

Stepping Stone

A boat sailed in. The Pilgrims landed.
It's how I—Rock—came to be branded.
The disembarkers stepped on me,
first footfalls toward their liberty.
I always keep this thought in mind:
What a big step for humankind.

Oh dear! Rock has really gone overboard! Open the foldout for the true story.

Rock Salt & Pepper

Who welcomed them?
I was the first.
Then came the tribes
with a great burst
of friendship, food,
community.
They gave these gifts
to the ones from the sea.
But everything
began with me!

Hold on a minute!

To be clear, Rock did not welcome any Pilgrims. That legend was invented 121 years after the landing, when a church elder named Thomas Faunce shared a story he allegedly heard as a child. No one knows for sure why Faunce spoke about a humble chunk of granite being stepped upon. Perhaps the story stuck because it offered a symbol of a new nation.

No large rock or stepping stone is mentioned in any of the travelers' journals or logs.

Rock perhaps should not have used the word "Pilgrims" to describe the travelers. Some of the immigrants called themselves First Comers, others used the names Saints, or Strangers. Only much later did the name Pilgrims stick.

Open here

On the Rocks

When colonists thought of breaking
from their motherland,
I was taken up quite roughly
by a local band.
Then I was severed,
cut right in two.
Some called it a sign
of what the colonists would do.

In 1774, when the colonists were thinking about cutting ties with England, a small group decided to move Rock to the town's meetinghouse.

Rock On

Another century,
another move.
I don't know
what they meant to prove.

My fame secure,
I broke in two,
dropped by a careless,
traitorous crew.

Leave No Stone Unturned

You'd think a national monument
would live an afterlife content.
Surrounded by a strong defense,
I waited for life to truly commence.
But with hammer, chisel, pick, and peck,
my life became a rocky wreck.

Rock is right about souvenir hunters. Because of those falls and chips off the old block, Rock became awfully stunted. Many of the pieces can still be seen in places like Plymouth Church in Brooklyn and the Smithsonian.

Set in Stone

Our country wrought in stone and fire,
itself a monument to admire,
suddenly tore itself in two.
But I—Rock—knew what to do.
I sent a signal of reunification,
and so we rebuilt our war-torn nation.

The Pilgrims, and those who came after them, built houses and monuments of stone, securing territory with guns and cannon fire. When the nation was being torn apart in the 1860s by a terrible civil war, it seemed as though the country would have to reinvent itself.

Rock Steady
1920

A big anniversary,
another big change.
Another housing
to rearrange.
Now placed in
a portico,
my life once more
is put on show.

I'm much too old
for all this moving.
What do they think
that they're improving?

In Rock's long life, its large chunks have been moved five times: in 1774, 1834, 1880, 1920 (into a temporary storage warehouse), and 1921 (into its new showcase—a neoclassical temple).

Rock Star 400th Anniversary 2020

Here's a party for all to share,
with boom and blast and rockets' red glare!

Loud huzzahs for four hundred years;
clapping and stomping amid loud cheers.
For me, of course, but there's something more.
It's for the country that I adore.

It's bigger than US. It's bigger than me.
It's really about nation and liberty.
The right to be, and the right to stay free.
And also the right to disagree.

Story can change the world, you see.
Take it from Plymouth Rock—that's me.
I've gone from glacier granite shocks,
to a place where Plymouth really Rocks!

Bibliography

Briggs, Rose, T. *Plymouth Rock: Its History and Its Significance*. Plymouth, MA: Pilgrim Society, 1954.

eReference Desk. "Massachusetts Early History." Joseph L. Ferguson. Accessed August 26, 2019. www.ereferencedesk.com/resources/state-early-history/massachusetts.html

Fritz, Jean. *Who's That Stepping on Plymouth Rock?* New York: G. P. Putnam's Sons, 1975.

History. "This Day in History." A&E Television Networks. Updated July 27, 2019. www.history.com/this-day-in-history/mayflower-departs-england

McPhee, John. "Travels of the Rock." *New Yorker*, February 26, 1990. www.newyorker.com/magazine/1990/02/26/travels-of-the-rock

Pelland, Dave. *Faith and Freedom: The National Monument to the Forefathers*. Monument Publishing, 2015.

Willison, George F. *Saints and Strangers*. Alexandria, Virginia: Time-Life Books, 1981.